PINTLALA'S COLD MURDER CASE

To Danny Shadix –
whose friendship across decades
continues to bless and enrich
my life and work
        –Gary Burton
        March 2019

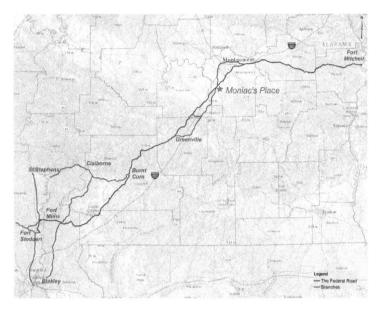

Map provided by Raven Christopher, archaeologist,
University of South Alabama

PINTLALA'S COLD MURDER CASE

The Death of
Thomas Meredith
in 1812

GARY BURTON

NEWSOUTH BOOKS

Montgomery

NewSouth Books
105 S. Court Street
Montgomery, AL 36104

Library of Congress Cataloging-in-Publication Data
ISBN 978-1-60306-436-1 (trade paper)
ISBN 978-1-60306-437-8 (ebook)

This book is adapted and expanded from the author's journal article,
"Pintlala's Cold Murder Case: The Death of Thomas Meredith in 1812,"
published in *The Alabama Review*, July 2010.

Printed in the United States of America

Contents

Buried not far from the banks of the Pinchona Creek in southwest Montgomery County, Alabama, and very near the site of Sam Moniac's (Macnac) Tavern on the Old Federal Road are the remains of Thomas Meredith. His murder in late March 1812 by militant Creek Indians inflicted a trauma on Meredith's westward-traveling family, a trauma for which they were unprepared. Exactly what happened to Meredith along the banks of the Pinchona Creek, punctuated by cypress knees and garrisoned by trees laden with Spanish moss, is cloistered in secrecy. Accounts of the incident vary; even the number of people in Meredith's party is uncertain.

What is clear is that the killing of Thomas Meredith quickly became a high-profile case, claiming the attention and energy of U.S. government officials.

The Meredith murder became even more significant as a result of two other incendiary incidents that occurred in 1812: William (Arthur) Lott, a former Georgia legislator, was killed in Macon County, and members of the Manley and Crawley families were killed or captured on the Duck River in Tennessee. This trilogy of atrocities became flashpoints that eventually ignited the Red Stick War in 1813.

Today, two centuries after the Meredith murder, two issues related to that incident need resolution. First, clarification related to the location of the crime is needed, and second (and more importantly) Sam Moniac's contention that the killing was accidental when an eyewitness contended otherwise needs to be examined. This paper seeks to address those two issues, while also providing an introduction to the man, Thomas Meredith.

THE OFFICIAL REPORT IDENTIFYING THE VICTIM

On April 6, 1812, William Eustis, secretary of the War Department, received a report announcing that Thomas Meredith Sr. had been murdered by militant Creeks. The official reporting of the murder came from Col. Benjamin Hawkins, who had been appointed by President George Washington in 1796 as General Superintendent of Indian Affairs and served in his post with prominence and distinction. Hawkins had lived among the Creek Indians, was especially familiar with the Creeks who lived in the Mississippi

Benjamin Hawkins, Indian Agent.

Territory, and was well traveled in the area that became central and south Alabama. During the presidency of Thomas Jefferson, Hawkins received federal support for implementing a plan of civilization among the Indians, encouraging their adoption of European agricultural methods.

In his 1812 report, Hawkins described the sixty-two-year-old Meredith as a "respectable old

man."[1] Other details, however, are not found in the official correspondence from Hawkins, who left much unsaid about the one
murdered on the banks of the Pinchona. What he did write was:

From Colonel Benjamin Hawkins.
Creek Agency, April 6th, 1812.

On the 26th ult. Thomas Meredith, Sen. a respectable old
man, travelling with his family to the Mississippi territory, was
murdered on the post road, at Kittome, a creek 150 miles from
this. Sam Macnac, a half breed of property, who keeps entertainment on the road, at whose house Meredith is buried, calls
it an accident. Thomas Meredith, son of the deceased, was an
eye witness, says, "there was murder committed on the body of
Thomas Meredith, Sen. At Kittome creek, by Maumouth and
others, who appeared to be in liquor; that is, Maumouth himself,
but none of the others. The company were all on the other side
of the creek, except my father and an old man. They fell on him
without interruption, and killed him dead as he was trying to
make his escape in a canoe, and sorely wounded the other, with
knives and sticks, so much so, that I fear we shall have to bury
him on the way." The Speaker of the nation and some of his
Executive council were with me, returning home, at the time I
received the communication, which I read to them, and directed,
on their return, to convene their chiefs, and cause justice to be
done without delay. Maumouth is an old chief, known to all of
us. Several travellers have passed and repassed since, and I hear
of no further interruption.[2]

---

1   Meredith's birth year was most likely 1750.
2   American State Papers, Indian Affairs, vol. 1: 809.

OVERVIEW OF MEREDITH'S DEATH

On the fateful Thursday, March 26, 1812, Meredith and his family were traveling through Creek Nation territory, located in the district of Alabama. Having safely traveled from the Fairfield District of South Carolina, where they had lived for two decades, the large Meredith family, like hundreds of families, was caught up in the euphoria of a new life in the Mississippi Territory. The compelling lure of land and the opportunity to start life anew held a powerful magnetism. Most of the journey of these families traversed the newly improved Federal Road or post road. The one-time horse path now accommodated wheeled vehicles and was heavily used. "Hawkins reported that between October 1811 and March of the next year, 233 vehicles and 3,716 people had passed his Indian agency on the Flint River, heading west."[3]

How many family members comprised the Meredith party is unclear. Meredith and his wife, Abigail, and most, if not all, of their children and their spouses, along with slaves, made the trip. Eventually, the family settled in Amite County, Mississippi Territory, although a few Merediths migrated on to Louisiana. Of course, they would do so without their patriarch.

One can only speculate about what provoked this confrontation between the militant Creeks and Meredith, culminating in Meredith's murder and leaving his unnamed traveling companion with life-threatening injuries. Contributing to the provocation, most likely, was the Federal Road itself. Traveling was arduous for those early migrants. Crossing creeks and rivers was challenging. Primitive bridges and causeways had been quickly and crudely constructed. "Timbers would be placed across the road and dirt packed between these logs to complete the causeways and keep horses from bogging

---

3   Henry DeLeon Southerland Jr. and Jerry Elijah Brown, *The Federal Road through Georgia, the Creek Nation and Alabama, 1806–1836* (Tuscaloosa and London: The University of Alabama Press, 1989), 39.

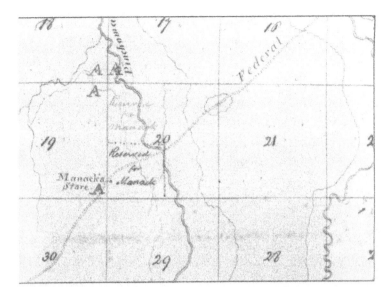

An early map of Pintlala.

to their bellies in the swamps."[4] The construction of the Federal Road allowed for easier travel and thus enabled the encroachment of white settlers, who threatened the traditions and heritage of the Indians. Every inch of progress in road construction was salt in the wounds of those who despised such sweeping changes.

Compounding the agitation over the road was Sam Moniac, who was at that time one of the wealthiest Métis (mixed-blood). He owned vast amounts of property and cattle and was the proprietor of a "house of entertainment" on the Federal Road. Moniac had typically been a supporter of the U.S. government. In 1790, he accompanied Alexander McGillivray to New York and put his mark as a signature on a U.S. treaty. Moniac's cooperation along with his success caused much resentment among the traditionalist Creeks, who distrusted the wealthy mixed-blood Indian because

4   Ibid., 23.

of his alliance with the intrusive federal government. These Creeks desired a speedy return to a bygone era, and on March 26, 1812, the two cultures clashed at the Pinchona Creek, which resulted in the killing of Thomas Meredith.

That day, most members of Meredith's party crossed the territory to the west side of the Pinchona Creek near present-day Pintlala. Lagging behind the larger party, having not yet crossed the Pinchona, were Meredith, his young son, and another man. These three met up with a group led by an old Creek Indian chief, Maumouth, whom Hawkins reported "appeared to be in liquor." The existing antagonism between the whites and the militant Creeks apparently provoked an intoxicated Indian chief to commit the crime, but there may be more to this story. If all but three in the Meredith party had crossed the creek earlier with all their gear and possessions, leaving Thomas Meredith, his son, and a companion to cross in a canoe, then it may have been that Maumoth and followers saw an opportune moment for harassment and taunting. Because much rain had fallen as a harbinger of the spring of 1812, perhaps Maumoth saw an opportunity to extort a high price from the Meredith clan by offering to assist them in the crossing of the Pinchona. While it is certainly speculative, the possibility of resistance by the Merediths may have ignited the fuse of the Creek Indians' anger. After all, the Meredith family had accumulated considerable experience in crossing creeks since leaving South Carolina. The Catoma and Pintlala creeks had been crossed before arriving at the Pinchona.

The experience the previous year of Margaret Ervin Austill is certainly instructive and enlightening when examining the Meredith murder. In 1811, as a young child, Austill traveled with her family from Washington County, Georgia, toward Louisiana. She recorded her memories of that trip, noting:

> Then the rain set in, not a day without rain until we crossed

the Alabama; there were no roads, and mud and water, large creeks to cross with slender bridges made by the Indians, which they demanded toll at high price for every soul that crossed a bridge, and often rather than pay, the men would make their negroes cut trees and make a bridge, which gave the Indians great anger, and they would threaten us with death.[5]

The attack on Meredith came just one year after Austill's experience, and a disagreement over paying tolls could have been a factor leading to the incident. Regardless of the motivation, the end result is clear. Meredith's young son, Thomas Meredith Jr., who witnessed the death of his father, stated that the perpetrator had killed his father, indeed, had "killed him dead."

CONFUSION ON THE LOCATION OF MEREDITH'S DEATH

In addition to uncertainty with regard to motive, contradictory information about the exact location of the murder has added to the confusion about this incident. Some of that confusion originated from the official report submitted by Benjamin Hawkins. Although Hawkins had resided in the Creek towns of Tukabatchee (now present-day Tallassee) and Coweta (near present-day Phenix City), he had moved the Creek Agency to the Flint River near what is now Roberta, Georgia.

Although Hawkins was the one to report the incident, he was far removed from the scene of the Meredith murder, a fact he acknowledged in his report, and perhaps because of his distance he mislocated the atrocity, writing in the April 6, 1812, letter reproduced earlier that it occurred "on the post road at Kittome, a creek 150 miles west of here."[6]

---

5 Margaret Ervin Austill, "Life of Margaret Ervin Austill," *Alabama Historical Quarterly* 6 (Spring 1944): 92–93.
6 American State Papers, n.p.

Kittome was a variant spelling for Catoma. Sam Moniac (Macnac), however, did not operate his tavern/store from the Catoma Creek. His business was located in present-day Pintlala, on the Federal Road near where it crosses the Pinchona Creek. Many variant spellings and pronun-

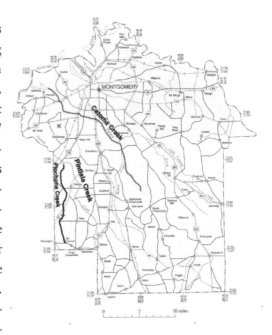

ciations exist for both the Catoma and the Pinchona creeks. Variant names for Catoma Creek include Auke Thome Creek, Catama Creek, Catatma Creek, and Kit-to-me Creek. Variant names for the Pinchona Creek include Pinchoma Creek, Pinchon Creek, Pinchonee Creek, Pinchorna Creek, Pinchunc Creek, and Pinchony Creek.

The problem with inconsistent spelling and variant names frustrated Thomas Foster II when he assembled *The Collective Works of Benjamin Hawkins, 1796–1810.* Foster chose to rely strictly on the phonetic spelling provided by Hawkins, conceding that "there are multiple spellings for almost every proper name. I prefer to leave the interpretation of place-name identification to the reader."[7]

In his records, Hawkins provided a tabular list of creeks

---

7   Thomas Foster, ed., *The Collected Works of Benjamin Hawkins, 1796–1810* (Tuscaloosa and London: The University of Alabama Press, 2003), xi.

TABLE 1:

Key Creeks in Montgomery County Near Pintlala

'Creeks Relative to the Post Road in the Alabama Territory'

Name	Length (Miles)	Width (Feet)	Terrain	
Ka-le-be	-	30	-	
Ke-bi-hatch-e	4	30	Lands post oak, clay, good stock range	
O-fuk-she	2	60	Post oak, small hickory, clay, red oak	
Noo-coose Chepo	2	8	Post oak, plains, clay, red oak	
Kit-to-me	14	60	Post, black oak, plains, clay	
Pilth-lau-le	7	20	do.	do.
Pinchunc	2	20	do.	do.
In-tuck-kee	4	10	do.	do.
Opil-thluc-co,	6	10	do.	do.
1st fork of	3	10	do.	do.
2d fork of	3	15	do.	do.

Found in Thomas Foster, ed., *The Collected Works of Benjamin Hawkins, 1796–1810* (Tuscaloosa and London: The University of Alabama Press, 2003), xi.

contingent to the post road in the soon-to-be Alabama Territory. A partial list is in Table 1, and the three major creeks in southwest Montgomery County are highlighted in the accompanying map.[8]

Given the heightened tension of the times and the prevalence of fear and paranoia among travelers on the Federal Road, the distortion of facts is easily understood. Without standardized spelling and pronunciation, misinformation would have easily been transmitted from the vicinity of the Pinchona Creek, where

---

8   Ibid, 855.

the murder occurred, to the Creek Agency on the Flint River in Georgia, where Hawkins resided.

Almost two centuries after the murder of Meredith, the confusion of location was perpetuated by Luke Ward Conerly in his study of Pike County, Mississippi,[9] the area in which some of Meredith's descendants eventually settled. Without the benefit of government documents, Conerly moved the site of the murder to the Georgia border. He wrote: "John Hart married Martha Meredith from Fairfield District, South Carolina. Her father was killed while moving to Mississippi, by an Indian at the Chattahoochie River, who threw a chunk at another man, striking him and killing him, which resulted in the Indian killing." The erroneous identification of the crime scene that began with the official report made by Hawkins was also perpetuated by Albert James Pickett, in his 1851 *History of Alabama*,[10] and General Thomas S. Woodward, in his 1859 *Reminiscences of the Creek, or Muscogee Indians*.[11]

Some clarification about the location is necessary to correct these errors. The point of the crossing of the Federal Road by Catoma Creek and the point of the crossing of the Federal Road by Pinchona Creek are about ten miles apart in distance, and the store or tavern operated by Sam Moniac was located only a few yards from the Pinchona Creek. Other sources about the incident clearly state that the murder occurred near Moniac's place of business: Henry Southerland Jr. and Jerry Brown noted, "Southwest

---

9   Luke Ward Conerly, *Pike County, Mississippi, 1798–1876: Pioneer Families and Confederate Soldiers: Reconstruction and Redemption* (n.c.: Southern Line Books, 2008). Reprint edition.

10   Albert James Pickett, *The History of Alabama, and Incidentally of Georgia and Mississippi, From the Earliest Period* (Republished by R. C. Randolph, 1896), 516, 518.

11   Thomas S. Woodward, *Woodward's Reminiscences of the Creek, or Muskogee Indians, contained in letters to friends in Georgia and Alabama* (Montgomery, AL: Barrett and Wimbish, Book and General John Printers, 1859), n.p.

Left and below: Iron and European and Creek pottery artifacts at site of Moniac's Store, Dr. Gregory Waselkov, principal investigator, Center for Archaeological Studies, USA, at Pintlala, May 10–11, 2011.

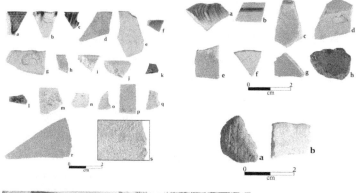

Pintlala Elementary School students at archaeological site in Pintlala, May 12, 2011.

of Colonel Wood's the next stop was Sam Manack's house, on Pinchony Creek";[12] Benjamin W. Griffith wrote, "The incident occurred near Sam Moniac's inn, which he kept for the accommodation of travelers on the post road, and Meredith was buried on the inn grounds";[13] and Gregory A. Waselkov asserted, "Thomas Meredith was murdered near Sam Moniac's stand in late March."[14] Waselkov provided cartographic evidence that locates Moniac's Inn near the Pinchona.[15]

MEREDITH'S LAST WILL AND TESTAMENT

After Meredith's death, his family moved on to settle in the Mississippi Territory, but the last will[16] and testament of Thomas Meredith Sr., dated September 15, 1808, was taken back to Fairfield County, South Carolina, and probated in Winnsboro on September 28, 1812. The will stipulated the payment of his debts and specified his slaves by name when designating the children who should acquire them. His bequests of real estate, livestock, feather beds, and furniture may have been typical of plantation owners of his day. An insight into Meredith's occupation is provided in the will, as he noted that his three sons should have "my blacksmith tools that each one may do their work."

The will provides a snapshot of the kind of life the Merediths had in South Carolina. They owned a modest estate with a plantation house complete with furniture and feather beds; stock comprised of horses, a mare, cows, hogs, and calves; and shillings and dollars.

---

12   Southerland and Brown, 94.
13   Benjamin W. Griffith, *McIntosh and Weatherford, Creek Indian Leaders* (Tuscaloosa and London: The University of Alabama Press, 1988), 80.
14   Gregory A. Waselkov, *A Conquering Spirit: Fort Mims and the Redstick War of 1813–1814* (Tuscaloosa: The University of Alabama Press, 2009), 88.
15   Ibid., 209.
16   The will transcript of Thomas Meredith may be viewed online in the South Carolina Archives: http://www.archivesindex.sc.gov, accessed May 7, 2010.

In his last will and testament, Meredith expressed his hope that his three sons (James, Thomas, and John) would give direction to the operation of the plantation, while parceling out the "things of this world" to his wife, sons, and daughters. The property distribution included six slaves: Jack, Isaac, Jacob, Jinney, and Marcus (affectionately referred to as "Old Marcus"). Intentions were expressed to keep the slaves together as long as circumstances permitted such an allowance.

LAND GRANTS TO MEREDITH, A WAR VETERAN

The land grants provide further insight into the life of Meredith and his family. The Meredith family's collective decision to pull up roots and transplant themselves in the territorial environment of the old southwest surely had been a difficult one. For the senior Meredith, much was sacrificed socially. In leaving South Carolina, this "respectable old man" left behind a one thousand-acre land grant (August 6, 1792) in Camden District, now Fairfield County. In addition, Meredith turned his back on 665 acres granted (May, 7, 1787) to him on Swift Creek in Kershaw County, South Carolina. The magnetism of a new life in the Mississippi Territory was strong enough to compel him and his family to forfeit the land and make the difficult journey deep into the old southwest.

Identifying the source of these land grants provides further information about Meredith. In all likelihood the land grants were a reward for his service as a Revolutionary War soldier. On July 10, 1784, Meredith presented a claim for payment to Thomas Baker, justice of the peace. The claim was certified on the same day by General Thomas Sumter, under whom Meredith had served as a foot soldier for almost four months of militia duty in 1781–1782 in Orangeburg, South Carolina. Additionally, Meredith served thirty-one days as a lieutenant under General Henderson at the battle of Four Holes (April 7 and 15, 1781).

At Four Holes, seventy mounted men led by Major George Cooper stormed the Loyalist post, taking twenty-six men captive. The British commander lost three men and was wounded himself. The Americans sustained the loss of one man, and two were wounded.

FAIRFIELD COUNTY RECORDS[17]

In addition to the will and land grants, Fairfield County court records also give insight into Meredith's life and involvements. The U.S. Constitution was yet to be adopted when the minutes of the court in Fairfield County, South Carolina, introduced the name Thomas Meredith. The county court began functioning in 1785, and the next year, Meredith appears and continued to appear, indicating that he was in the center of much litigious activity.

On January 25, 1786, Meredith was the plaintiff in a lawsuit in which he brought charges of slander against William Graves, James Graves, and Hugh Means. The somewhat thorny and complicated matter also included a charge against Meredith by Isaac Love. Unfortunately, no record exists concerning the nature of the charges. Resolution to the charges and countercharges did not occur until three months later in May when, over a four-day period, the court issued its ruling regarding each person involved.

On May 9, petit jurors were seated with John McKinney as foreman. In the case of *Meredith v. William Graves*, the jury found in favor of Graves. The next day, James Graves was dismissed from Meredith's suit, and Meredith was compelled to pay the court costs. The third day brought an interesting approach on the part of Meredith and his attorney. When the court was asked to rule on the matter of slander by Hugh Means (mistakenly spelled Minor in the court record), Meredith challenged McKinney's role as foreman.

---

17   Brent H. Holcomb, comp., *Fairfield County, South Carolina, Minutes of the County Court, 1785–1799* (Easley, SC: Southern Historical Press, 1981), 10–21, 65, 82–89, 92–94.

For whatever reason, McKinney was replaced by Richard Gladney, and the jury was impaneled. This time the jury ruled in Meredith's favor and awarded him one pound sterling. Very quickly the defense attorney sought an arrest of judgment, which was granted. The court then required that both the defense and prosecuting attorneys resume their argument the next day.

If there were drama to any degree in the back-and-forth litigation, it was not present the next day when the court referred the case to mediators John King and Ralph Jones. The court determined that the judgment of these two mediators was to be final, and their decision must have been agreeable to Meredith, for two of his children would soon marry the children of mediator Ralph Jones.

Subsequent years would find Meredith performing his civic duty as a juror for the Fairfield County Court. The tenor of the times can be seen in two judgments rendered by the juries on which Meredith served. On June 14, 1793, William Hollis and others were brought to trial, having been indicted for hog stealing. Those indicted other than Hollis were exonerated, but Hollis was found guilty and ordered to pay fifteen pounds by the next Tuesday at one in the afternoon. If not paid, he would receive "25 lashes on his bare back at the public whipping post." The next day, June 15, 1793, Meredith participated in rendering a verdict against John McBride, who had been indicted for larceny. He was found guilty and was given jail time until July 8, at which time he was to receive "ten lashes on his bare back" and was expected to pay the entire costs of the sum stolen.

On a side note, in all the times of service of Meredith as the plaintiff, defendant, or a juror, he was in a courtroom presided over by members of the Winn family, whose most prominent member was Richard Winn. Fitz McMaster, in a *History of Fairfield County*,

South Carolina,[18] noted General Winn's valor in battle. While commanding a regiment of refugee militia, the firing became intense, and Winn turned to General Davis, exclaiming, "Is not that glorious?" For Winn, the glory of the battlefield was later exchanged for life of public service, and the village of Winnsboro, named for his family, became the county seat.

MEREDITH, THE BAPTIST[19]

While court records from South Carolina provide some information about Meredith, early nineteenth-century Baptist documents offer even more clues. Minutes from the Charleston Baptist Association reveal that five months before Meredith was killed he attended that association's meeting, which was held in Columbia. When representatives from twenty-seven churches convened in Columbia on Saturday, November 2, 1811, Meredith was present as a messenger from Wateree Creek Baptist Church. He, along with fellow messenger James Hart, attended this annual event. The church's pastor, Rev. Ralph Jones, was absent from the meeting, most likely because of his poor health.

The Wateree Creek Church typified many of that area and era. While the church had existed for many years, with the first meeting house built in 1770, it had relocated from its original site to an area about five and a half miles south of Winnsboro. The church was identified as a branch of the Congaree Church until 1803, when it was accepted as a "member of the Charleston Baptist Association with the name Wateree Creek Baptist Church." This request for membership was made by Jones as early as 1799, and because Jones had spent much of his life as pastor of the church, many referred

---

18 Fitz Hugh McMaster, *History of Fairfield County, South Carolina, from "before the white man came" to 1942* (Columbia, SC: The State Commercial Printing Company, 1946).

19 Minutes, Charleston Baptist Association, 1803–1811.

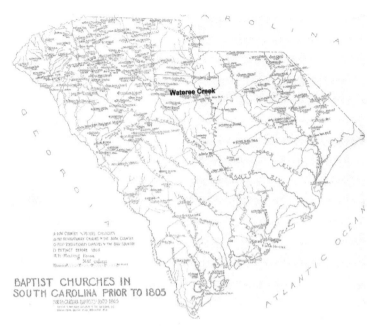

BAPTIST CHURCHES IN
SOUTH CAROLINA PRIOR TO 1805

Meredith was associated with the Wateree Creek Church,
highlighted in this map of Baptist churches in South Carolina.

to the church as the Ralph Jones Meeting House.

The Wateree Creek Church, according to tabular records, had
an average of between fifty and sixty members during the first
decade of the 1800s. The church often contributed financially to
the missionary fund and (less often) to the education fund of the
association.

The associational records indicate that Thomas Meredith rep-
resented the Wateree Creek Church for first time as a messenger
in 1803, and he attended the meeting every year from 1807 to
1811, with the exception of the year 1808. The summary record
of churches consistently indicates that Meredith was a layperson
in the Wateree Creek Church. He is never listed as a minister, and

ministers were specifically designated in the associational records.

Each year during the annual gathering of church representatives, Meredith found himself in the company of notable Baptist leaders, including the Rev. Dr. Richard Furman, who was pastor of First Baptist Church, Charleston, and founder of Furman University. Furman served as the association's moderator for many years. Other notable Baptists who made significant contributions and with whom Meredith rubbed shoulders were Dr. Jonathon Maxey, who had served as the second president of Brown University and who would be tapped to serve as president of the University of South Carolina; William B. Johnson, who was pastor of the Beaufort Church, served for twenty-seven years as president of the South Carolina Baptist Convention, and who, in 1845, was elected as the first president of the Southern Baptist Convention; and Jesse Mercer, who was a prominent Baptist minister and founder of Mercer University.

Meredith joined these and other Baptists in conducting business typical of early associational life: receiving and reading letters from corresponding associations, drafting circular letters, admitting new churches, hearing sermons, alerting churches to religious hucksters, and pronouncing moral judgments on social functions. Meredith surely heard Furman inform constituents about mission efforts among the Catawba Indians, including the building of a school. This work was led by the Rev. John Rooker. Furman shared with the messengers that funding for the school and mission work was tenuous, but he told them that he had approached the state's governor, Jared Irwin, who encouraged the association to ask for the state's financial assistance. Apparently progress was made at the school, for Rooker provided optimistic reports, including his 1810 report in which he produced "satisfactory specimens of pupils' writing."

The 1811 meeting of the Charleston Baptist Association, the last Meredith attended, launched a study to assess the practicality of establishing a seminary; condemned the social practice of dancing schools and balls; and proclaimed the second Wednesday of March as a day of humiliation, fasting, and prayer among churches. By mid-March of that year, Meredith and his family would be well on their way, traveling the Federal Road into the heart of the Mississippi Territory, and by late March, Meredith would be dead, murdered near the Pinchona Creek.

AN ATTEMPT AT RESOLVING THE MEREDITH CASE

The murder of Meredith appears to be an open-and-shut case. There was a perpetrator, a victim, and an eyewitness. Those responsible for the crime were apprehended and executed. There was official documentation that brought closure to the crime. Yet, on an unofficial level, one unresolved matter remains.

In the correspondence from Hawkins to Secretary of War Eustis, the Indian agent wrote, "Sam Macnac, a half-breed, of large property, who keeps entertainment on the road, calls it an 'accident.'"[20] Moniac's assertion was made in spite of the fact that Thomas Meredith Jr., age nine, gave an eyewitness account of the intentional murder of his father by the Creek Indians.

The question then is why Moniac would declare the killing of Meredith to be accidental. His rationale may have reflected a confluence of motives. First, on a practical and elemental level, Moniac knew that news of a murder near his tavern could possibly lead to rampant hysteria and ultimately adversely affect his business. Talk of the murder of a traveler in such close proximity to his place of "entertainment," where travelers found lodging, food, refreshment for horses, and other supplies, could potentially close his business down.

Second, Moniac's motives for asserting the killing was accidental

---

20   Kathryn Braund postulates that "accident" was a euphemistic expression used by the Creeks for a private matter as opposed to one officially sanctioned.

may have been influenced by his own personal struggle with alcoholism. Ten years after the Meredith killing, in the aftermath of the Red Stick War and the defeat of the British, Moniac's alcoholism had accelerated to the point that it had destroyed his life and left him destitute. While the loss of some of his property and possession must be attributed to his loyalty to the United States government, which made him hugely unpopular in some Indian circles, Moniac's alcoholic behavior resulted in the loss of his remaining property. With impaired judgment, Moniac participated in a series of bad business deals until he was left virtually destitute. Evidence of Moniac's behavior is documented in a letter from his relative, David Tate, to Sam's son David Moniac, who was serving as the first American Indian cadet at West Point.[21] Emphasizing the urgency of the situation, Tate advised David Moniac to return home and salvage what was left of his father's possessions. Sam Moniac conceivably could have been involved in a personal struggle with alcohol, at least in the nascent stages, at the time of Meredith's death, and his alcoholism could have led him to be sympathetic to the behavior of Maumoth, who was "in liquor" at the time of the incident.

Third, the fact that Moniac's place of "entertainment" was on the Federal Road near the Pinchona Creek opens up the door to some interesting speculation. Perhaps Moniac felt some degree of responsibility for Meredith's death because Maumouth and his party had acquired their "liquor" from Sam Moniac's tavern.

Finally, cultural tensions were already high at the time Meredith's death occurred. As one of the most prominent Métis in the Creek Nation, Moniac doubtlessly believed that hostilities were rising against those who had expressed an allegiance with the United States. Because of his support of the federal government

---

21   David Tate letter and receipt, SPR26, Alabama Department of Archives and History.

and because of his full acculturation to the lifestyle and traits of the whites, militant Creeks viewed Sam Moniac as the epitome of everything that threatened their traditions and heritage. The idea of blending cultures had resulted in clashing cultures. Harassments and agitation to resist any form of white influence was something to which Moniac was no stranger. As one of the wealthiest Métis, he had every reason to suggest that the Meredith atrocity was accidental because he knew that an investigation of the incident, followed by friendly Creeks pursuing, apprehending, and executing other Creeks, would deepen the cultural divisions and put him at risk. Ultimately, the labeling of the killing as a murder could result in the loss of everything Moniac had accumulated and could lead to the decrease in his standing within the Creek Nation itself. Of course, Moniac's fears would eventually become reality.

Seventeen months after the murder, on August 2, 1813, a deposition was sworn by Moniac before Harry Toulmin. In summarizing the events of March 1812, Moniac stated, "Being afraid of the consequences of a murder having been committed on the mail route, I had left my home on the road, and had gone down to my plantation on the river."[22]

An Interesting Similarity

The experience of traveling the Federal Road when tension and fear were almost palpable was shared by the Rev. Lorenzo Dow and his wife, Peggy. Dow was from Connecticut and was probably the first Protestant minister to travel into the Mississippi Territory for religious purposes. Along with his wife, Dow had been to St. Stephens, the territorial capital of Alabama, and they then traveled further north on the Federal Road, stopping along the way at

---

22 Sam Manac deposition, SPR26, Alabama Department of Archives and History.

Peggy Dow.

Fort Mims. This fort, which deeply impressed the Dows, was destroyed during the 1813 Red Stick War, thus helping us to date the travel of this couple in the years just previous to 1813.

The Dows continued their journey into what became central Alabama and entered Creek territory. Their encounters along the Federal Road and their brief stop at Moniac's tavern in present-day Pintlala illustrate the foreboding conditions of traveling on the recently cleared road. Peggy Dow wrote of their experiences in *Vicissitudes:*

At last we came in sight of a Camp, which would have made my heart glad, but I feared lest it was Indians; yet to my great satisfaction, when we came to it we found an old man and boy, with what little they possessed, going to the country that we had left behind, and had encamped in this place, and with their blankets had made a comfortable tent, and had a good fire. This was very refreshing to us, as we were much fatigued. We made some coffee, and dried our clothes a little—by this time it was daylight; we then started on our way again. I thought my situation had been as trying as almost could be, but I found that there was others who were worse off than myself.

We came across a family who were moving to the Mississippi—they had a number of small children; and although they had something to cover them like a tent, yet they suffered considerably from the rain the night before; and to add to that, the woman told me they had left an aged father at a man's house by

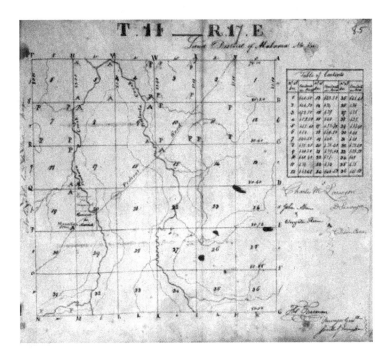

The Thomas Freeman map plat.

the name of Manack, one or two days before, that she expected
he was dead perhaps by that time. They were as black almost
as the natives, and the woman seemed very much disturbed at
their situation. I felt to pity her—I thought her burthen was
really heavier than mine. We kept on, and about the middle of
the day we got to the house where the poor man had been left
with his wife, son, and daughter. A few hours before we got
there, he had closed his eyes in death—they had laid him out,
and expected to bury him that evening; but they could not get
any thing to make a coffin of, only split stuff to make a kind of
a box, and so put him in the ground![23]

23   Peggy Dow, *History of Cosmopolite: or the writings of Rev. Lorenzo Dow. . . To
     Which is added, the "Journey of Life" by Peggy Dow* (Cincinnati, OH: Applegate

Peggy Dow's records on this incident were first printed in 1814, and her experiences obviously took place before the outbreak of the Red Stick War. The Dows certainly could have been in Moniac's tavern shortly after Meredith's murder, and her description of events involving a death at Moniac's seems to have occurred about the time of the Meredith incident. Is it possible that she was referring to the unnamed person who was injured when Meredith was killed?

The Dows, like most families that journeyed westward, often traveled with other family groups, and like most families during this period, fears about personal safety were part of that journey. For the entrepreneur Sam Moniac, reducing fears and conveying a sense of safety would have been in his best interest, for he had a business to protect. Thus, the hasty burial at Moniac's tavern may have been the result of his desire to dispose quickly of the problem and not simply because there was no wood available for a coffin. While that is only speculation, what we do know from Peggy Dow's account is that there were at least two burials at Moniac's "house of entertainment."

HIGH-PROFILE ATROCITIES

The other known fact is that over a span of a few weeks two other murderous incidents provided enough combustible material to ignite momentous tensions and fears in the region. Of course, other dangerous confrontations occurred between white travelers or settlers and militant Indians, but none of these confrontations rose to the same level of notoriety as did the massacre of the Manley family and the murder of Arthur Lott. News of these two other atrocities were merged with the story of Thomas Meredith's murder on the Pinchona Creek in Alabama, and together these stories swept like a rapidly spreading prairie fire, resulting in increased insecurity

---

and Company, 1855), 129.

and paranoia among those who were migrating into the southwest and those who had already homesteaded.

MURDERS ON THE DUCK RIVER
AND THE CAPTURE OF MARTHA CRAWLEY

The Manley massacre took place about six weeks after the murder of Meredith. News of another massacre at the hands of militant Creeks resulted in a concussion of shock waves that rocked the frontier. In mid-May 1812 on the Duck River in Western Tennessee, five Indians invaded the home of Humphreys County resident Jesse Manley. The Indians murdered and scalped seven people, five of whom were children, and took Martha Crawley captive.

As if the Duck River crimes were not horrific enough, newspaper accounts reported the event with embellishment and sensationalism. The public was already smoldering with anger when the *Tennessee Herald* reported graphic details of the Manley home invasion, calling it "the unequalled scene of hellish barbarity," and thus inflaming and enraging even the calmest of souls. According to the newspaper's account, Jesse Manley and John Crawley were away from home when the Indians saw one of the Manley children outside the house. The Indians approached the house and grabbed the child, "whom they tore to pieces with their dogs and scalped." The account continued:

> with savage fury they now forced the door, and commenced a scene of still greater barbarity. They snatched Mrs. Manley's child, only eight days old, from her, scalped it and threw it into the fire place, yelling at a horrid rate. An indiscriminate butchery of the children now took place before their mother; five children were scalped and murdered, they keeping Mrs. Manly alive as the last victim of their cruelty. After shooting her, they scalped her, and committed unheard of cruelties on her body. They then left the

house, taking Mrs. Crawley along as prisoner.[24]

Tennessee Governor Blount, in a June 25 missive to Secretary of War William Eustis, attempted to bring clarity to Mrs. Crawley's status. Blount had learned through an informant "that she has been severely whipped, exhibited naked in circles of warriors, who danced around her; and that at present she is at Tuckabatchee, beating meal for the family to whom she belongs." Sometime in late June, Martha Crawley escaped her captors, and in a subsequent deposition, she did not mention being severely whipped, stripped of her clothes, or made the object of dancing. She did indicate that she was tied to a tree on the first night of captivity and that, at one point, "she was ordered by one of them to stir a pot of hominy that was then on fire."

During this period, politicians and military leaders, typified by that of Andrew Jackson, skillfully made use of incendiary rhetoric to advance their ambitions. Jackson was more than eager to invade the Creek Nation, as indicated in his missive to Governor Blount of Tennessee:

> . . . the sooner the[y] can be attacked, the less will be their resistance, and the fewer will be the nations or tribes that we will have to war with. It is therefore necessary for the protection of the frontier that we march into the Creek Nation, demand the perpetrators, at the Point of the Bayonet, if refused, that we make reprisals, and lay their Towns in ashes. . . . I only want your orders, the fire of the militia is up, they burn for revenge,

---

24   A date for the reporting of this atrocity by the *Tennessee Herald* is unknown. However, the report was picked up by other publications across the country. *The Lady's Miscellany, or The Weekly Visitor: For the Use and Amusement of Both Sexes* 15, no. 9 (Saturday, June 20, 1812).

and now is the time to give the Creeks the fatal blow, before the[y] expect it.[25]

THE MURDER OF ARTHUR LOTT

The final of the three atrocities in 1812 was the murder of Arthur Lott (who was later misidentified as William Lott). Lott departed Montgomery County, Georgia, traveled via the Federal Road, and was murdered at Warrior's Stand in Macon County, Alabama. Having served several terms in the Georgia General Assembly, his influence in Montgomery County, Georgia, was pervasive to the point that the functions of the county court and jail were moved to his plantation in 1797.

This trilogy of atrocities roused great fear and resulted in much rage among the white settlers. Although justice was exacted in all three murderous events, bringing Creek Indians into subjection became a controlling obsession. Yet looking at the context in which these murders took place provides additional insight. In early 1812, when all three incidents occurred, the United States was on the threshold of war with Great Britain, and the Indians were believed to be in alliance with the British. Since the Revolution, the tie between the British and Indians had been cemented. For their part, the Indians resented the encroachment of westward-moving white settlers, while the British agents working with the Indians, despite the fact that they had received precise orders not to agitate the Indians toward war with the settlers, did in fact promise them military assistance if war did occur. Thus, this alliance between the British and the Indians along with the imminent British intrusion added to the hysteria of the times.

---

25 John Spencer Bassett III, *Correspondence of Andrew Jackson* (Washington, D.C.: Carnegie Institution, 1926–1933), I: 226.

The Antecedent Influence of Tecumseh

One last factor to be considered is the influence of Tecumseh, the Shawnee chief. In October 1811, six months before Meredith was murdered, Tecumseh traveled to Tukabatchee, Alabama. Having been immensely influenced by the British in Detroit and working with Indians in Canada and the Great Lakes region, Tecumseh, in tandem with his brother Tenskwatawa, moved southward attempting to build a pan-Indian Confederacy that would use military force to resist all expressions of white settlement and European influence. Inciting and agitating young Indian warriors, Tecumseh ignited the Creeks, challenging them to throw off any vestige of military and cultural dominance of the white man. That cultural dominance and white movement into Indian territories were epitomized by the civilization plan of Hawkins and the on-going construction of the Federal Road.

By the time Tecumseh and Tenskwatawa arrived in Alabama, they had built a loose alliance of Indian tribes. Tenskwatawa, called the Prophet, brought tremendous spiritual fervor and fanaticism

Left, Tecumseh. Right, Tenskwatawa.

to the movement, and Tecumseh encouraged confrontation and militant assault on anyone and anything that proved a hindrance to a return to pre-European culture.

The mounting hostility on the part of the Indians, again, must be viewed in the larger, more compelling context of an imminent war with the British. Henri, while depending on the work of Edmunds, stated, "Tecumseh accepted gifts of arms and supplies from the British and was led to believe vague promises that, if he could form an anti-American confederacy of all the tribes, the British would synchronize an assault with an Indian uprising to drive out the common foe."

In a retrospective on a speech made by Tecumseh to five thousand Creeks convened at Tukabatchee in the fall of 1811, Hawkins, in 1814, wrote:

> Tecumseh, in the square of Tuckabatchee, delivered their talk . . . kill the old chiefs, friends to peace; kill the cattle, the hogs, and fowls; do not work, destroy the wheels and looms, throw away your ploughs, and everything used by the Americans. Sing 'the song of the Indians of the northern lakes, and dance their dance.' Shake your war clubs, shake yourselves; you will frighten the Americans, their arms will drop from their hands. . . . Has this proved? Go to the fields of Talledega, and New–yau–cau, and see them whitened with the bones of the Red Clubs.[26]

By the late spring of 1812, white travelers and settlers had a keen awareness of the danger posed by Tecumseh's leadership, and the hostility his words and actions aroused along with information about the three Creek murders, the anticipation of war with Britain,

---

26 Florette Henri, *The Southern Indians and Benjamin Hawkins 1796–1816* (Norman: University of Oklahoma Press, 1986), 265.

and the threat of further alliance between the Indians and British were the causes of great anxiety.

JUSTICE ADMINISTERED BY THE CREEKS

Given the unrelenting fear caused by all these factors, white leaders, such as Benjamin Hawkins, moved quickly to administer justice following incidents of violence. In the immediate aftermath of Meredith's death, Hawkins charged friendly Creeks with the assignment of apprehending, punishing, or executing those responsible.

Beginning in 1790, the United States government had entrusted the administration of justice among the Creek Nation to the Creek Indians, believing that sharing this responsibility would build trust and create a continuance of autonomy for the Creek Nation. While there may have been earlier agreements between the government and the Creeks, the enabling authority for surrendering the administration of justice to the Creek Nation is found in the 1790 Treaty of New York.[27] That year, a contingency of Creek chiefs led by Alexander McGillivray made their way to the nation's capital. Among the chiefs was Sam Moniac, whose signature is found on the treaty. The treaty, brokered by Secretary of War Henry Knox, included Article 8, which spelled out the terms for indigenous justice:

> If any Creek Indian or Indians, or persons residing among them, or who shall take refuge in their nation, shall commit a robbery or murder or other capitol crime, on any of the citizens or inhabitants of the United States, the Creek nation, or town, or tribe to which such offender, or offenders may belong, shall be bound to deliver him or them up, to be punished according to the laws of the United States.[28]

27   Kathryn Braund observes that there were earlier expressions of Creeks administering justice within agreements brokered by the United States.

28   For the entire treaty, including articles see http://avalon.law.yale.

In his April 6, 1812, missive to the Secretary of War, Hawkins noted that when he received word of the Meredith murder, the speaker of the Creek Nation was in his company, along with members of the speaker's executive council. Hawkins's letter indicates that he immediately instructed them to convene a meeting of their chiefs as soon as they returned home, and he asked them to "cause justice to be done without delay." Then Hawkins added that Maumouth, the only one drunk in the party of perpetrators, was well known to members of the executive council and their chiefs and was a prime suspect in the crime.

The demands for justice among white settlers intensified following the murder of Lott and the atrocities related to the Manleys and Mrs. Crawley. In both cases, Creeks were convened and authorized to administer justice. Over the summer of 1812, fear and paranoia gripped those who were traveling on the Federal Road as did a persistent preoccupation with apprehending and punishing those who were guilty of these crimes of notoriety.

Although Hawkins was criticized for not acting swiftly and forcefully, he had sought the help of two dependable operatives, Billy McIntosh of Coweta and Little Prince of Broken Arrow, and Hawkins also dispatched his assistant, Christian Limbaugh, to speak with McIntosh about the urgency of apprehending the murderers. Hawkins apparently chose wisely, for the persuasive powers of these men prevailed. Little Prince sent a mixed-blood chief, George Lovett, with Limbaugh and McIntosh to talk with Big Warrior. Apparently the chain of influence was crucial in organizing a response among the Creek chiefs to the recent crimes.

Correspondence between the chiefs and Hawkins indicated the resolve of the chiefs to deal with the murderers. On June 7, they wrote a letter that stated:

edu/18th_century/cre1790.asp, accessed May 6, 2010.

We the kings, Chiefs and Warriors have assembled in our
Council House and taken into consideration the danger which
threatens our land; we have unanimously agreed that satisfaction
shall be given without delay for the murders committed in our
land. We have appointed three parties, one party started last
evening, the other two this morning, in pursuit of the murderers
of Thomas Meredith and Arthur Lott, who were murdered on
the post road. The parties have received their special orders not
to stop until they have punished these murderers.[29]

Later, Billy McIntosh traveled to the town of Hopoithle Micco,
which was where the "leader of the Banditti" who was responsible
for Lott's murder had sought sanctuary. McIntosh invaded the town
and shot and killed the criminal.

Meredith's killer was also swiftly punished. Hawkins, in correspondence to William Eustis dated July 28, conveyed the news
of imposed justice: "Being on the road, I have just time to inform
you that the Indian who murdered Meredith, at Kittome, was put
to death on the 19th; making in all five executed on the demand
for satisfaction."[30] Hawkins's report brought some relief to the
mounting tension.

On August 24, Hawkins wrote triumphantly to the Secretary
of War that others in the party that killed Meredith had been
punished, noting that "the chiefs had six murderers put to death
for their crimes on the post road and to the northwest and seven
cropped and whipped for thefts." Five days later, the Indian agent
wrote again, reporting that a total of eight Indians had now been
executed for Meredith's murder. On September 7, Hawkins notified
Governor Mitchell of Georgia:

---

29   Merritt B. Pound, *Benjamin Hawkins, Indian Agent* (Athens: University of
        Georgia Press, 1951), 215.
30   American State Papers, Indian Affairs, IV: 812.

Left, William Eustis, Secretary of War. Right, Georgia Governor David B. Mitchell.

The proof I have of the satisfaction taken for the murder of Meredith and Lott and the stabbing of one of Meredith's companions is such as is customary here. The Chiefs sent with armed parties to execute them, returned and reported to the Executive Council when and where they executed them, and this report is sent to me by the Big Warrior and Mr. Cornells. I have received three formal reports of the success of their efforts to fulfill their promises mailed to me, the last of the 29th ult. They have executed up to that date eight, and have cropped and whipped seven. Hillaubee Haujo and three other were for murders at Duck River and Northwestwardly.[31]

---

31   C. L. Grant, *Letters, Journals, and Writings of Benjamin Hawkins: 1802–1816* (n.c.: Beehive Press, 1980), 617.

CONCLUSION

Thomas Meredith, a "respectable old man," a veteran of the Revolutionary War, a Baptist churchman, a South Carolina plantation owner, and a blacksmith by trade, died on the banks of the Pinchona Creek in 1812, nearly two hundred years ago. Beginning just a few weeks after his death at the hands of a group of militant Creeks, conflicting accounts of the murder surfaced. Today, two troublesome issues related to his murder have been identified, and hopefully, resolution to those two issues has been offered. First, since 1812, confusion has existed about the location of Meredith's death. Second, the issue of whether the killing was a murder or an accident has also been addressed.

The question of misidentification of location is the most easily answered. Hawkins, unfamiliar with the area, simply made a mistake. The confusing names of creeks and the variant spellings contributed to this understandable error.

The second issue is more complex. Understanding why Sam Moniac would call Meredith's death an accident when Meredith's son, an eyewitness, claimed it was intentional is puzzling, but Moniac's response does provide insight into his personal struggles and also the tension of the times. What would become central Alabama was already embroiled in a cultural clash, and fear of change was a daily part of the lives of both the Creeks and the white settlers.

Official records help in the understanding of the context, but those records do not capture or communicate the grief and pathos of the Meredith family. Shocked by the sudden, violent death of their patriarch, the family now faced starting a new life in a new place without his guidance. Surely, the burden of loss colored every dynamic of their lives as the family of Thomas Meredith moved farther west and eventually homesteaded in Amite County, Mississippi Territory. His death perhaps can be seen too as a small harbinger of the great tragedies imposed on Native Americans, upon whom

This historical marker is located at the intersection of the Federal Road and Cloverfield Road in Pintlala.

forced relocation brought about sweeping cultural changes.

In September of 1812, the last will and testament of Thomas Meredith, written in 1808, was probated in the Fairfield County Court, South Carolina. Representatives of the Meredith family returned to witness this legal proceeding and to sell Meredith's South Carolina property. What must it have been like for them to return the way in which they had once before traveled? What must it have been like for them to pass by the place in which their father had been senselessly murdered?

In September 1812, the Meredith family members journeyed along the Federal Road to South Carolina, knowing that hostilities were more intense, that war was closer to a reality, and that Sam Moniac's "house of entertainment" now stood guard over the grave of Thomas Meredith. Within a year's time, the Red Sticks would lay waste to Moniac's property; he would never recover from the loss of seven hundred cattle, two hundred hogs, forty-eight goats

Pinchona Creek, Montgomery County, Alabama.

and sheep valued at $5,060, a cotton gin, two thousand pounds of cotton, thirty-six slaves, and several houses.[32] The brief return of representatives of the Meredith family to their home in South Carolina in order to probate the will of their patriarch may have been done with the assurance that those accused of the murder had been executed.

Everyone loses in violent, cultural wars. Giant oak trees still line the Pinchona Creek and stand as silent sentinels guarding the unmarked grave of Thomas Meredith.

---

32   Claudio Saunt, *A New Order of Things: Property, Power, and the Transformation of the Creek Indians, 1733–1816* (Cambridge University Press, 1999), 260.

Index

CPSIA information can be obtained
at www.ICGtesting.com
Printed in the USA
BVHW040847010319
541326BV00016B/169/P

9 781603 064361